Homemade Christians

A GUIDE FOR PARENTS OF YOUNG CHILDREN

written and illustrated by Nancy Marrocco

COLLINS   NOVALIS

Collins Liturgical Publications
8 Grafton Street, London   W1X 3LA

Collins San Francisco
Icehouse One — 401, 151 Union Street,
San Francisco, CA 94111-1299

Distributed in Ireland by
Educational Company of Ireland
21 Talbot Street, Dublin 1

Collins Liturgical Australia
PO Box 316, Blackburn, Victoria 3130

Collins Liturgical New Zealand
PO Box 1, Auckland

Novalis
PO Box 9700, Terminal,
Ottawa, Ontario   K1G 4B4

Wood Lake Books
PO Box 700, Winfield,
British Columbia   V0H 2C0

Copyright ⓒ1985 and 1987, Novalis,
St. Paul University, Ottawa, Canada.

This edition first published 1988.

Collins ISBN 0-00-599138-2
Novalis ISBN 2-89088-331-0

Printed in Hong Kong
by South China Printing Co.

Library of Congress Cataloging-in-Publication Data

Marrocco, Nancy
     Homemade Christians.

     1. Child rearing -- Religious aspects -- Christianity.
     2. Parent and child -- United States. I. Title.
HQ769.M297   1988   261.8'35874   87-24259
ISBN 0-00-599138-2 (Collins)   ISBN 2-89088-331-0 (Novalis)

Homemade Christians

Dedicated,
with very much love,
to my family and friends

Being a
Christian Parent

is like getting rosebushes to produce roses.

There is a child in your care-- Gregory or Lorie or Margaret or Jim--one of our very youngest Christians. Like a rosebud, your child needs special caring in order to blossom and grow.

This book is for you, the rose gardener. (Although it is designed especially for those whose children are under six years of age, its message is for all parents.) It is written to help you explore the strengths and resources
already available
to you
for the awakening
and cultivating
of your child's
faith.

You, the Christian parent,
   have started out with what
     is already growing,
       already precious and holy. . .

I
You are a Treasure

God knows you.
One of God's own children
   has been entrusted into your care
   because you are precious and important;
      God knows who you are.

You are reading a book about raising children
         as Christians.
   Why did you pick it up?

Somehow, somewhere, you have a desire that your child be Christian. In that desire, there are some powerful resources.

You picked up this book. Keep remembering why.

The desire to give a child what's good is a Christian desire.

You were already looking for good things to give
your child when you were searching for a
good name. And, probably, your search began
before you ever even saw your newborn child.

Try to recall the names you were considering for your
new baby. Why did you favor certain ones
and not others?

Mrs. M. liked the name 'Lorie' because
she thought it sounded like the name
of a nice person. Mr. B. wanted
something 'traditional, not fluffy';
he liked the name 'Margaret'
because of the strength and
substance he saw in it.

If you look very carefully into
your own search for just the
right name, you may get a
glimpse of your desire at work...

What were you trying to give your child?

The desire to give a child what's good
is a Christian desire.

Now, think about the crib, and perhaps the room, which you prepared for your new arrival.

Maybe you got a basket with a good mattress. Maybe you bought a blanket (a warm one? a soft one? a brightly colored one?) You might have painted the room a new color.

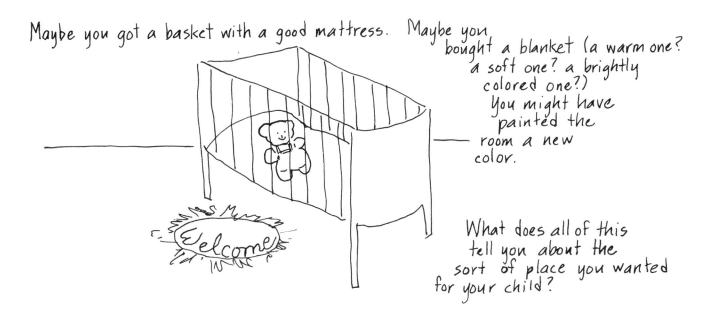

What does all of this tell you about the sort of place you wanted for your child?

What you were really doing was carving out a special place in which your new baby could feel warm, safe and happy. Again, you were gathering good things for your child.

Who are the people in your young child's life?
To whom have you introduced
him since he was born?   Why?

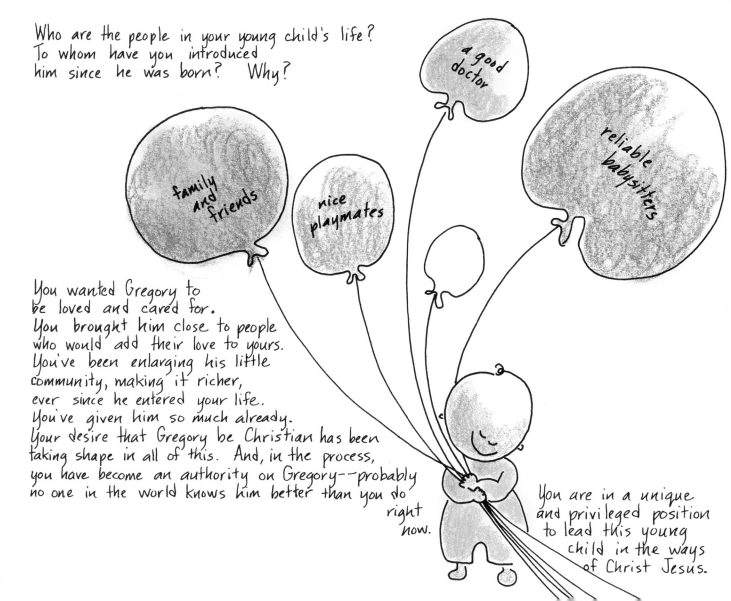

family
and
friends

nice
playmates

a good
doctor

reliable
babysitters

You wanted Gregory to
be loved and cared for.
You brought him close to people
who would add their love to yours.
You've been enlarging his little
community, making it richer,
ever since he entered your life.
You've given him so much already.
Your desire that Gregory be Christian has been
taking shape in all of this. And, in the process,
you have become an authority on Gregory--probably
no one in the world knows him better than you do
right
now.

You are in a unique
and privileged position
to lead this young
child in the ways
of Christ Jesus.

II DON'T BE AFRAID TO DO THIS WORK

Maybe you will admit
that your desire is strong--but
you might fear that your faith is weak.

Faith is a growing thing, in all of us. You have faith.
Otherwise, you would not care about awakening it in Stephen.

Faith belongs to God, to the Mystery of love.
We don't know all of God's Plan, just yet; the study
of how faith develops and grows is rather new.
Even newer is the question of how faith
gets started in very young children, like your Stephen.

When this precious child was given to you,
there were no detailed instructions attached, as there would be with a
paint-by-number set where the spaces are already marked and the colors already
chosen.

Instead, this God of faith and splendor provided you with the paints and
the brush, so that you could mix the colors
and make the strokes.

Don't be afraid of the uncertainties. They are also
the doors to possibility, opportunity and discovery:

Behold,
I do new things
and now
they shall spring forth.

I will make
a new way in the wilderness, and
rivers in the desert.

(cf Isaiah 43:19, 20)

No one knows exactly how to lead a child to God. But, there are definite
signposts, and we are always coming to
new insights.

Your own faith is itself a gift for Stephen,
a vital part of his journey with God.

You are already
an active, living, changing,
vital and ongoing part
of Stephen's growth in faith
because YOU already
believe in God.

This is the excitement
in raising Christian children.

II YOU ARE NOT ALONE

God's Love

At this very moment, it is not only you who are helping Dan come to God. Take heart.

Did you know that Dan's life with God had already begun, even before you came into the picture? God has been there, loving him, since before the beginning of time. God waited, watching over this little child as he secretly took shape in the womb, wanting Dan to live in order to shower him with good things.

God is watching over Little Dan right now, even as you read this book.

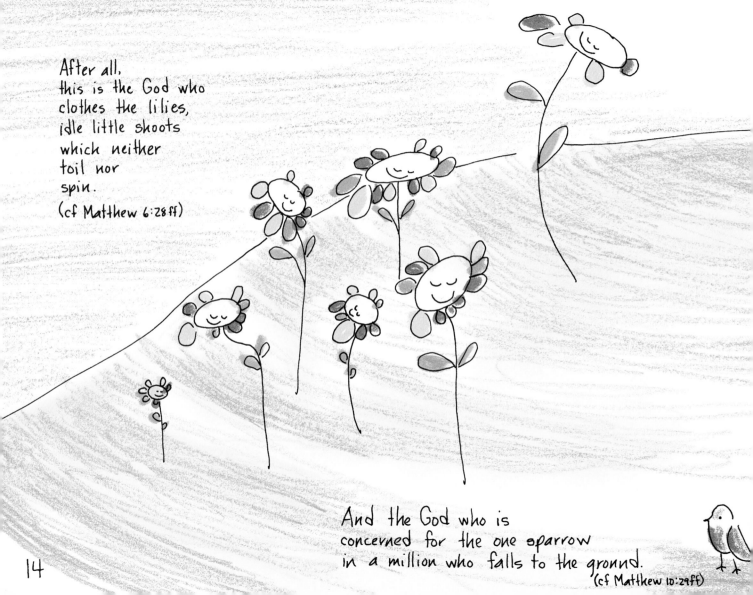

After all,
this is the God who
clothes the lilies,
idle little shoots
which neither
toil nor
spin.

(cf Matthew 6:28ff)

And the God who is
concerned for the one sparrow
in a million who falls to the ground.

(cf Matthew 10:29ff)

14

From beyond the stars,
from within the quiet of the womb,
from inside Dan's own heart,
God has been speaking to this one so beloved . . .

Precious child of My Heart,

You and I are as one.
Your hopes, your dreams, your rhythms are Mine.
My breath yours. My strength, yours.
I created you because I have always loved you.

Precious child,
sparkling jewel on the seashore,
you are Mine, radiant in My sight.
Remain in My love.
I know you — you are My heart and I, your love.
No one may take the light, the glory, the peace
I give you.

I love you powerfully and in ways unknown to the
world. The seed grows in the dark
and I have loved you forever.
Carry forth My creation in your dreams,
your hopes, your colors, your life.

Be My victory.
Dance My dance. Sweet child of light,
let Me redeem the world through you.

15

By the time Dan entered the world,
   he was already filled with light and life...

We come to realize that this child,
young though he is, may respond to God's love.

Responding to God's love is prayer,
and the prayer of young children can be surprisingly rich.

When God and Dan encounter each other, Dan touches a deep peacefulness,
the kind of peace
which fills his entire being.
He may stay in that moment with God
for a long time.
If he has words, he may speak — simply — but the joy of God's presence
will make his words both holy and profound.

Dan's capacity for prayer should not be underestimated.

And neither should God's desire
to wrap this tiny child
in the mysteries of love,
speaking to him in tones so deep that only the very young could understand.

We always want to speak our joy to the ones we love, telling them how wonderful they are. When Dan hears the Good News of Jesus Christ, his heart will sing. And, quite naturally, the song of his heart will be praise of God. This is prayer.

Create a safe, quiet space for Dan. Pray with him as often as you can. Lead him into the love of Jesus and let him encounter this wondrous God of ours.

Sometimes, Dan's prayer will be silent. Sometimes musical. It might be a gesture he makes or a picture he draws. It might be a single word, or two. If God's love leads Dan to sing, it might even make him want to dance.

He might want to repeat a prayer you've taught him. (But, take care. Encourage him to express himself in his own unique way before giving him someone else's words, even your own.)

Prayer happens in many different ways,
probably more than we know.
But, it is genuine as long
as it allows Dan to
receive God's love
and respond to it.

Remember that Dan was
born loved, and that he has always
been nourished by God's love.

Dan is already turned toward God, just as a green leaf turns toward
the sun.

The Christian Community

It was the wonder of such a green leaf and of such a warm sun that Jesus Christ came to proclaim. And He commissioned all of His followers to continue His proclamation:

The Lord Jesus told us to go out and tell the WHOLE WORLD about His Father's LOVE

(cf Mark 16:16)

So that absolutely everyone
would hear this
most wonderful
news, He
gave His
own
Spirit.

And those who
were filled with it
received
power.

When they told the Good News, people of every language hear

And, around this Word of Love,
there grew up a community
of Christians, one which
has now grown to include
Dan.

Dan has always been a
child of God; because
you have chosen for him
to be baptized, he is
now a Christian child
of God.
That means he is supported
by the faith and graces and hopes
of the entire Christian community.

By being baptized in Jesus Christ, Baby Dan has entered a special
relationship with Him and with all of us who still believe in Him
and try to follow Him.

Dan may not realize yet that he belongs to this believing community,
or that it's called the Church. He still doesn't know very many
of these people, but we're all there,
holding him up,
bringing him forth
with our love and prayers.

21

You are a Christian parent;
you also have been commissioned
by Jesus Christ.

You He sends to the very youngest
of His people.

He asks you
to take this small child,
already bathed in God's own love,
and to lead him more deeply into this Holy Mystery.

And to you, the Lord Jesus gives His Spirit.
You are able to tell Dan about God's love in very special ways.
Some are so mysterious that neither you nor I could explain
them.

But there are
many ways to
tell the Good News
of Jesus Christ, and
there are some we
can explain, at
least a little. Helping
Dan to make connections
is one of them.

As you lavish your love on him,
leading him into the good things
of life,
you can CONNECT LOVE WITH GOD and you
can CONNECT YOUR HOME with the CHURCH.

Dan already experiences God's love through you,
and is already surrounded by God's good gifts. You can show
him that good things come to us from God. You can help him
to connect the love of your home
with the love
of the Christian
community.

Light, water, stories, music, song and people are some of God's most precious gifts. They are also very accessible -- we find them at home and at Church.

The next few chapters
show how these can be ways of telling your child
the Good News of Jesus Christ.

Where activities with
very young children
are described, the exact ages
cannot be given. This is
because your child
is unique.

And because it is you
who are the best
judge of the proper
moment in which
to introduce a new idea
or to make a new gesture.

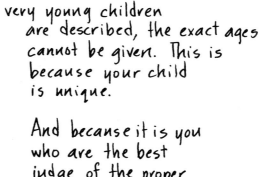

IV LIGHT

Martha knows about the light.
She squints in the sun, falls asleep at night
when the light's on in the hall.
And fireworks thrill her.

Tell Martha that Jesus is the Light of the world. . .

"... a light
that shines in the dark,
a light
that darkness
could not overpower."

(John 1:5)

25

As you are getting ready for Christmas,
light the four candles of the Advent Wreath.
Two purple, then one pink (a note of joy),
then one more purple.

She'll see the light growing.
Tell her that Jesus
is coming like that.

At Christmas,
celebrate.
Light candles at
Christmas dinner.
Light up the
whole house.

Hold Martha in front of the tree,
and look at the lights with her.
Put the figure of the Christ Child into your
crèche and move a big lamp so that
it's right over your stable.

Bundle her up one night
and go out to see the
stars together.

Then, tell her
about the star
over
Bethlehem.

Connect lights with celebrations. Use candles
for thanksgiving, anniversaries, homecomings.
On Martha's birthday, light up her cake with
candles. (Even one, if it's her first, will
be a spectacular display.) Let her
blow them out and then start all over again.
Before she goes to bed, look out the window
with her to see if there's a sunset.

When you pray together, light a candle.

27

If you can, take Martha with you to an Easter Service.

On the night before Easter,
we gather together in the darkness,
waiting for the first light of dawn.

In anticipation of the Easter "Sonrise",
we light a candle,
a light of new promise against the darkness.
This light we pass from person to person until, finally,
the darkness is thrown back by a sea of lights and we
draw closer to the
new day of the
Risen Lord
Jesus Christ.

We celebrate
Easter.

Sunday
was the day of the first Easter.
Every Sunday, in church, we celebrate the Lord's Resurrection again,
in a new way.

When you take Martha to church with you, show her
the candles. (If you are early enough, you can sit at
the front and she can see them being lit.)
We keep lighting candles; Jesus' love keeps
lighting up the world.
And we try to do the same.

Look up at the windows with her
to see the colors of light shining through
the stained glass. Go to the windows
and see the different colors close up.

Martha
knows about light.

Tell her that Jesus is all the light in the world,
and all the colors of the sunset.

30

▽ water

When our ancestors were faltering in the desert,
God revived them with water:

"...splitting rocks
in the wilderness,
quenching their thirst with unlimited water,
conjuring streams from the rock
and bringing down water
in torrents."

(Psalm 78:15-16)

31

Probably, few things will delight and intrigue young Joseph more than his bath.

It's warm and safe, and you're there with him. He can splash and play and discover all sorts of wonderful things to do with water.

And what joy it is for him to run under the cool sprinkler on a hot summer's day, or to tear along the beach.

Water is so common, and yet so appealing.

A blessing on those
who put their
trust in Yahweh...

They are like a tree by the waterside
that thrusts its roots to the stream: when
the heat comes, it feels no alarm,
its foliage stays green...
— cf Jeremiah 17:7-8

Teach Joseph to love water.

Connect it with life and joy and Mystery.

Let him enjoy water
while enjoying something or someone else:

put two straws into a cup of water and let him drink it with
his friend Toby.

Take Joseph to church when there's a baptism and get him
to watch what happens. Tell him that, when he was
baptized, water was poured over him like that,
and that water comes from God.

Watch the rain with him.
Let him water the plants with you.
Make sure he sees how it picks them up--even if
you have to let them wilt a bit first.

Take Joseph to lakes and rivers and
waterfalls and streams and little puddles.

Tell him that, in making the world, God made water part of almost everything.
Even Joe's lemonade is mostly water.

When Joseph is very thirsty, give him a long cool
drink and tell him that coming to Jesus
is like coming to water when
you are very thirsty . . .

" . . . anyone who drinks
the water that I shall give
will never be thirsty again:
the water
that I shall give
will turn into a spring inside him,
welling up
to eternal life."

(John 4:14)

35

Connect water and life with Jesus.

Tell him that Jesus was baptized in a river. And that water was poured over Him, just as it was poured over Joseph.

When you say Grace together at supper, thank God for the food AND for the water.

VI STORIES

Little Ruth loves stories and books. She loves the pictures and the colors.

Sometimes, she flips pages just for the fun of it.

Connect STORIES with the BIBLE.

But, most especially, she loves stories when you're there with her, either holding her with a book on your lap, or whispering your own stories to her in bed at night.

The Bible is a collection of books, all telling the same story, all inspired by God, but each in a different way. It's the story of God-with-us, through the ups and downs of our history. Some biblical authors told the story with poetry, others as history, as instructions for worship, or as narrative, prayer or song.

Connect STORIES with
JESUS.

Tell Ruth that
Jesus Christ came to tell us
stories of His Father and how very much His
Father loves us.

People flocked from all over just to hear Him. (They wanted to be close to Jesus, this magnificent story-teller, just as Ruth wants to be close to her favorite story-teller, you.)

Then they wrote down the stories of Jesus, the Good News which we call the Gospel.

Add the Bible to Ruth's collection of books.

And do two things with it: make the Bible special, but also make it touchable.

Special

Tell Ruth
that the stories in the Bible are
so important to us that we listen to them
whenever we go to church.

Show her the lectern set aside for the Bible. Draw her attention
to it during the readings.

At home, give the Bible a special place. And connect
it with especially loved things. One shelf could be
kept especially for the Bible--and for one or two
of Ruth's most treasured things--
those which she herself has
chosen to put there.

Tell Little Ruth
that when we read the Bible together, at church or at home, God is with us in a special way:

" *Where two or three
meet
in My Name,
I shall be there
with them.* "

(Matthew 18:20)

Touchable

Let Ruth hold the Bible, and carefully flip its pages. (If she is too small just yet, you could flip a few for her.) When you read from the Bible or pray by it, do that where she can see or hear you.

Let her put the Bible on the dinner table for special occasions. Read a verse or two from a psalm as a way of saying Grace, and let her hold the book while you read. As you are close to Ruth with other books, be close to her with the Bible.

Although the Bible is for every one of us,
the Biblical authors were not writing with little children in mind. Scripture is
addressed to an adult community.

While she is still so young, only certain passages of the Bible will have direct
meaning for her. Therefore, make your selections very carefully:

1. Use only one or two short verses
   at a time.

2. Choose passages which strike a deep
   chord in her, especially those which
   appeal to her need for protection
   and security.

   You can discover the right chords
   by watching Ruth and by talking
   with her as you are reading. What captures her
   attention? What does she ask to hear a second time?
   What makes her ask questions? What makes her
   quiet and peaceful? For example, it has been found
   that young children respond in a very special way to the
   parable-allegory of the Good Shepherd.

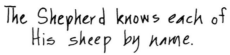

The Shepherd knows each of
His sheep by name.

They are safe and peaceful
with Him.

42

(John 10:1-16)

3. Choose passages which use concrete images, as in The Pearl of Great Value (Matthew 13:45-46), The Parable of the Yeast (Luke 13:20-21), The Loaves and Fish (John 6:5-14), etc.

You can use concrete things to make the stories come alive for Ruth.
Take out a shiny bead and let her hold it while you tell the story of the Pearl.

When she is with you in Church during communion, remind her of how the loaves and fish were shared among so many. If you're cooking rice or baking bread at home, show her the before and the after: something which begins so small but which grows to be very big.

(Like God's Kingdom)

4. In general, try not to use passages which emphasize people or events about which Ruth is still too young to know.

Would you use a "Children's Bible" with Ruth, or would your own adult version be better?

A Bible written for children is of good quality if:

1. It maintains a deep reverence for the biblical message, being respectful of this in the way it's written;

2. its illustrations are appealing to Ruth, calling forth in her a response to the message;

3. and its language is within her understanding.

On some occasions, your own Bible might be the best book to use with Ruth. At other times, and for other reasons, you might prefer to use a Bible written for children.

VII

Music and Song

Timothy hears music.

And he reacts to it. He bounces up and down to tunes on the radio. Sometimes he'll invent a song of his own.

And some of his favorite songs are most likely the ones he's heard you singing.

45

Take Timothy to church when there is music.
Watch him. What makes him stop and
listen, even for a second?

Is there any
musical instrument
which seems to
affect him more
than others?

What is _he_ hearing?

Connect the music at church
with the music of your
home. Bring home the
sounds and songs he
likes best. Either sing
him the songs yourself, or play a
recording.

"Sing Yahweh a new song!
Sing to Yahweh
all the earth!"
(Psalm 96:1-2)

And, when you and Tim are in church again,
tell him that our love for God is making us sing, and that when we sing to
God, we
are prayin

VIII People

When you bring little Terry
to church with you,
you are bringing her
into the midst of
people—
lots of them.

The celebration may seem very long to
Terry. Look for opportunities to connect her with
what's happening, especially with the people and what they're doing.

Boys and girls may be helping, and there may
be special singers or musicians.
There will be people of all ages, praying.
And there will be one person in particular
who is leading us,
gathering our prayers together
into a single
strong voice.

As people are greeting each other,
or giving each other a sign of Christ's peace,
    someone might reach out to touch Terry.

That may be a special moment of closeness with
    other Christians. Don't let
    her miss it -- with her
    little hand in yours,
    reach out and touch
    back.

Then, at home,
you might all hold hands
    around the table
        during Grace.

Communion is a special moment
for the Christian community.

In this moment, we get closer to Jesus, together.
Tell Terry that Jesus wanted everyone to
be close to Him. One day, He asked
especially that children be allowed
to come to Him (Mark 10:13-16).

Hold Terry in your arms
as you receive the Bread
and, still holding her,
tell her that the two of you
can be close to
Jesus, together.

If there is a song during communion, focus
her attention on the hymnbook, the music,
the choir, the singing community.

Remind Terry that, when we sing to Jesus,
we're telling Him that we love Him.

You have been bringing Terry
  into the midst of people
  ever since she was born.
  And these people have been
  enriching her life.

Help her to see the richness of the Church
  in its people: the celebration of God's power and promise
  and love is happening in us, the people,
  in all our words and actions of
  praise and thanks through
  Jesus.

IX Growing in God's Sacred Garden

God has planted
the sacred garden.

You have been given a
precious rosebush, already
planted for you in God's own garden, already being showered with God's own water
and light.

What God wants you to do is tend
to the flowering. Because you are
a treasure, you are being trusted
in the sacred garden with these
little seedlings. God is relying on
your caring and
tending... and
watering...
and
cutting...

Andrea is not always sweet and sunny. Often, she is cranky and rebellious. But she needs your love and guidance through her rebellions too.

God created roses with thorns.

Andrea's little thorns are there for a reason. When she turns red and screams her lungs out, she may be a little less appealing. But, there is a definite purpose in that scream.

It is by way of the thorns also that she learns to love and to be loved.

You already know how to take care of Andrea.

You feed her the right things.
You protect her from the summer sun
and from the cold winds in winter.

And you are hugging and kissing her
into life
all the time.

Your Andrea is love-able. She responds to love,
and grows. You are building on that very same
love to awaken her to God. You are connecting
love with God and your home with
the Church.
Using light. Using water. Using
song.

Making connections.

The gardener
        must do certain things in a certain way
            to get the rose bushes
                to flower.

                    When you bring Andrea
                        to the water
                        or to the
                            light,
                        teaching her to
                    sing
                to the God who
            cherishes her so deeply,
        you are using
    special skills in a special way.

Know your own skills and talents.
The more you know them, the better you can use them.

---

1. You DELIGHT in Andrea.

You love it when she smiles; and it's wonderful when a stranger stops to say Hello, or just to admire her. You celebrate her every little triumph, even her first tooth.

REJOICE with Andrea in all the gifts and talents the Lord God has given her.

---

2. You WATCH Andrea.

You see (almost) everything she does. You know where she goes. You watch her face to see how she'll like her new breakfast cereal.
You listen to her new words and to her many little requests.

You are in tune with Andrea.

STAY IN TUNE. You are learning about
Andrea's growing faith by watching
it take shape in a million
little ways
every day.

See what she likes, what she
doesn't like. Listen to the
things she says.

Notice who or what she puts into
her pictures. Ask her why.

Listen to her questions.
See what she notices when she's at church.
When is she still? When is she jumping?
Stay in tune with Little Andrea.

3. You SURROUND her with good things.

Like the rose gardener, you set up and maintain the best conditions for growth to take place. You give Andrea support and plenty of encouragement when she tries to take her first step.

When you present her with her
first peas and carrots,
you wait till she's
in good humor.
Then, you smile and play her into swallowing that first important bite.

You give her toys which will teach her new things-- colors, numbers, patterns, movement.

KEEP SURROUNDING HER with your FAITH. Pray where she can see you or hear you. Let her see the reverence with which you pick up the Bible.

Take her to church with you
when you most want to
and are best able.

You are Andrea's first and most important model of a Christian.

How you live your own faith affects her much more profoundly than anything else you could possibly say or do.

4. You GUIDE Andrea.

Away from the corner of the table so that she won't bump her head. Towards her little cousin so she'll make friends. Towards her grandfather for a big hug.

And you lead her through all her funny little garblings to her first intelligible words.

You are also GUIDING HER TOWARDS GOD. Take her by the hand and lead her.

Take her to the church some time when it's empty. Let her touch things.

Let her roll around on the carpet,
and look up at the windows.
Teach Andrea a little prayer--maybe
one of your own, maybe not.

Tell her the story of how Jesus
was born. Tell her about the
day He welcomed the children
and little babies (Mark 10:13-16).

Keep connecting good things with Jesus.

Keep guiding her towards Him.

5. You are exceedingly PATIENT with your young child.

You take her with you for a walk to the park or a trip to the store, knowing full well that she'll stop every two minutes to look at this or to touch that.

But, as much as you can, you wait; and you let her explore. Just as you wait, seemingly forever, to get her to swallow those last few bites of mashed potato.

With the same quiet patience, you WAIT as Andrea COMES TO GOD.

Keep giving her opportunities to touch this God of glory and peace, and to be touched by God.

Keep guiding and encouraging.

But then, step back and wait. She needs room to respond to the Lord. To grow.

Trust that
something is happening inside her little head or heart,
even when she is perfectly silent—or perfectly obnoxious.
Believe that, when she prays, something is happening
between this tiny child and God Most High.

You can lead Andrea towards God. You can awaken faith in her
and help it to grow. But you can't do HER praying.
You can't live her relationship with God FOR HER.

Let Andrea encounter God.

Just be there
to open the
door for her,
and to
wait quietly
        outside.

You are the rose gardener.

You don't have to create the roses
    or pull open the petals.

Your only concern is to help the bushes
    to the water and the light.

Then, sit back to savor their growth and magnificent
                                        beauty. . .

62

I Take HARVEST for Granted

"Yes, as the rain and snow
come down from the heavens and
do not return without watering the earth,
making it yield and
giving growth to provide
seed for the sower and
bread for the eating,
so the word that goes from my mouth
does not return to me empty
without carrying out my will and
succeeding in what
it was sent to do.
(Isaiah 55:10-11)

We are all growing in God's sacred garden.
You and Gerard both,
cherished. This God
of power and majesty
showers both of you and all of
us with light, grace and
peace unending.

63

Jesus Christ is the very center of God's love. We who are Christians gather together at this center, and we call it Church. Here, we love and pray and go forth to work in the name of Jesus, our Lord and Savior.

Keep Little Gerard with you at this center.
Teach him and guide him and pray with him.

And, as you both are growing,
    keep your hearts
        in tune with Jesus.

    And slowly, let go of that little boy,
        that treasure first given to you by God,

            trusting
                that he is falling into
                    the arms of Jesus,
                        into the
                        heart
                        of God
                    most tender,
                most loving,
            most holy . . .

" . . . I am with you always, yes even to the end of time."

(Matthew 28:20b)